Rick
Springfield

by Simone Gillianti

Wanderer Books

Published by Simon & Schuster, Inc., New York

Rick Springfield

Design by Stanley S. Drate/Folio Graphics Co., Inc.

Manufactured in the United States of America

10 9 8 7 6 5 4 3 2 1

WANDERER and colophon are registered trademarks
of Simon & Schuster, Inc.

Also available in Julian Messner Library Edition

Library of Congress Cataloging in Publication Data

Gillianti, Simone.
   Rick Springfield.

   Summary: A biography of musician and actor, Rick
Springfield, an Australian import who came to the United
States and became a superstar.
   1. Springfield, Rick, 1949-   . 2. Singers—United
States—Biography. 3. Actors—United States—Biography.
[1. Springfield, Rick, 1949-   . 2. Musicians.
3. Actors and actresses] I. Title.
ML420.S766G5   1984   784.5'4'00924 [B]   84-9073
ISBN 0-671-53103-4 (lib. bdg.)
ISBN 0-671-53102-6 (pbk.)

Contents

Early Days in Australia

Richard Lewis Springthorpe was born in Sydney, Australia, on August 23, 1949. He did not become Rick Springfield until many years later. Unlike many performers, he did not really pick his own stage name. When his musical career began, and he started getting mentioned in the papers, the reporters who wrote about him kept making the same mistake: Every time he said "Springthorpe," they printed "Springfield." In the end, he stuck with it.

His mother and father, Eileen and Norman, called him by his nickname, "Ziz." He blames no one for that but himself. As a small child he pronounced his own name "Zizzy."

Rick and his brother Mike got to know the small continent of Australia pretty well, especially cities such as Melbourne and Sydney. Their dad was a career Army colonel, M.B.E. (M.B.E. stands for Member of the British Empire. Australia used to be a British colony, like America before the American Revolution.) The Springthorpes moved from one Army base to another, never settling in one place for more than two years.

Kids with parents in the armed forces are often called Army brats. They lead a different life from that of most kids, since they spend so much time in and around Army bases. Having a parent in the Army can make you feel as if you had signed up yourself!

It was a difficult life for a sensitive young boy. Every time Rick got comfortable, his father announced that he had been restationed. Before he knew it, Rick became the new kid in town again. Have you ever moved away from a town and friends you liked? It can be hard to move even once. It takes a long time for a new kid to prove himself or herself and get to know people. Rick's shyness did not help much. By the time he had made friends, it was time to leave.

For much of Rick's childhood, his family lived in Melbourne, in several different neighborhoods. In big cities, every neighborhood is like a separate town. Living in one part of the city does not prepare you for living in the other parts. For Rick, Melbourne was a rough place in which to grow up.

The Springthorpes were a very close family. They never had enough time to make friends, so they made friends with each other. No one else provided companionship, fun, love, or entertainment. They did not even own a television set until 1958. Evenings were spent around the piano, with Norman playing while the family sang Broadway show tunes. The songs of *Carousel* and *South Pacific* were favorites, and Rick still remembers the words to those songs.

Norman's love of music and the family chorus are special memories for Rick. Years later, he thanked his dad for those memories in a special way. After Rick moved to America, he and his parents communicated by cassette tape. The tapes were much better than letters. Sometimes Norman even sang a song for his son. One Christmas, Rick took all the tapes into a studio and transferred his singing dad onto a real record. The finishing touch was a homemade cover with a picture of Norman and Eileen on front. They were so proud and happy when it came in the mail.

Rick loves animals. He never had enough pets as a child, so when he moved to America, he made up for lost time. His pets have included a lamb, an eel, a lizard, chickens, dogs, cats, and parrots. One of those dogs is the one he has now, the famous Ron. Ron is almost as much of a star as his master, ever since

Rick made him one by putting him on the covers of two of his albums.

Another thing Rick made up for after moving to America was the insecurity of never owning a home. The Springthorpes did not own a house until Norman retired. When Rick settled down in America, he needed a place of his own, with lots of room for his animal friends! So, he bought a house.

A Bad Move

The Springthorpes' biggest move took them far from their homeland. Nine-year-old Rick packed up his things as he had many times before, but this time there was a difference. The Springthorpes were moving to a new country. Norman had been restationed in England.

What a huge change this was for Rick and Mike! There are lots of differences between England and Australia. Australia is isolated. It is far down south. The climate is dry and warm. England is close to the rest of Europe. The climate is very damp and chilly.

There are some similarities between the two countries. Soccer is popular in both, even though Australian soccer has different rules. Another common interest is cricket, a game that is a little bit like baseball.

Have you ever seen an Australian TV program? You may have noticed some differences between an Australian accent and an English accent. When you first hear them, they sound alike. After you listen for awhile, you can hear a thousand differences. It is like comparing someone from New York to someone from Mississippi.

Any hope Rick had of fitting into his new environment disappeared when he met the kids in his new school. He was labeled a dumb foreigner. "In England, I was the Australian pig, the new kid with the funny accent," he told *Seventeen* magazine. "It was really traumatic. Because of the country schooling I had, I knew less than the English kids my age, and I got cut to pieces."

The cruel teasing hurt Rick, but his classmates did not stop there. Rick got beaten up over and over again. He learned to fight, not because he wanted to, but so that he could defend himself. Now he has a brown belt in tae kwon do, which is a kind of karate. Back in 1958, however, he was easy prey for bullies.

It is always sad when people are prejudiced against other people. Those boys might have liked Rick if they had gotten to know him. They may even now be among the millions of people who buy his records, and yet they did not want to know him just because of the way he talked.

Rick used music to forget the bad times. In a way, music was a new thing to him. Until recently, Australia never had a lively pop music scene. Since Australia is expensive to visit, many bands never played there. The local bands were years behind the rest of the world because they never saw new musicians. These days Australia is catching up. Olivia Newton-John, Men At Work, and Rick Springfield have helped put Australia on the charts. But when Rick lived and grew up there, the music scene was not very active.

In England in the late '50s and early '60s, music was much more important. New bands and new sounds popped up every week. Everybody talked about the Beatles and the Rolling Stones, young men with long hair who left a trail of screaming teenagers behind them.

Before the '50s, most of the songs on the pop charts were made by older people. Kids bought the same records as their parents did. Then, when rock 'n' roll took over, the kids had their own music, but it was still made by older people. Bill Haley, the man who sang "Rock around the Clock," played for audiences young enough to be his children.

The '60s changed all that. Now the musicians were part of the same generation as their fans. Some of those bands, such as the Rolling Stones and the Kinks, are still around today. The Beatles were Rick's big influence. John Lennon and Paul McCartney are

Rick and Andy Gibb, another successful Australian export.

still his favorite songwriters. If you listen to some of the early Beatles albums, such as *Meet the Beatles,* you can hear the same songs that excited Rick so much when he was your age.

Rick developed other interests too. He always says that if he had not been a musician he would have been a veterinarian. Once when a fan asked him what other jobs he would enjoy, he talked of his interest in archaeology. Egyptology especially fascinates him.

The past interested him in other ways also. English literature was one of his favorite subjects in school. He loved the old, creepy horror classics of Edgar Allan Poe, such as "The Pit and the Pendulum." Rick is still fond of horror movies. He remembers riding his bike around sand pits in an English town called Woking, a town he liked because H. G. Wells used it as a landing spot for his imaginary aliens in *The War of the Worlds.*

Dreams of invading aliens and kings' tombs were not as stirring as music. Because of the music he heard in England, Rick's five years there changed his life.

Some Dreams Come True

Rick fulfilled his passionate love of music when the Springthorpes moved back to Australia. His parents gave him his first guitar for his thirteenth birthday. "I proceeded to saw it in half, trying to make an electric guitar out of it," he told *Teen* magazine. "Then I painted it bright red. My parents weren't too thrilled about that, so I had to buy the next one myself. Later they helped me buy my first electric guitar."

Practicing the guitar and singing became his main pastime. Rick is a self-taught musician. Learning to play by yourself takes work and dedication, because there is no one to tell you how to correct your mistakes, and sometimes you do not even know what your mistakes are. A few years ago, Rick took some singing lessons. He is always trying to improve his voice, but he feels confident about his guitar playing. After all, he has played professionally for over a decade.

Old problems mixed in with the joy of playing the music he loved. The fights continued, even though he was no longer the "dumb foreigner." One day he found himself in a new neighborhood. He walked up to some local kids to say hello, and they thrashed him. Things he wanted to do were off limits. Concerts tended to be full of thugs. He and his friends risked beatings for just going to a show.

**Rick in 1974.
What a difference
ten years make!**

At the age of sixteen, Rick had a band called the Jordy Boys. The name was taken from one of Melbourne's tough suburbs. Rick told *Circus* magazine about his first professional gig: "It was for a party, for ten pounds [about fifteen dollars]. We had been playing the guitar together and copying Beatles records and everything. We got together with another guy and his brother and played old tunes, the ones that were current then. We played all night, till they told us to stop."

Rick's parents were not happy about his interest in music. It took a long time for them to accept it. After all, musicians have an unstable life. Eileen and Norman loved their son and were concerned about his future. They did not want to see him make a mistake. If Rick got hurt, it would hurt them too.

Eileen and Rick began fighting constantly. Norman had to step in and make peace. After awhile he convinced Rick to stop fighting with his mother, but it took a long time to iron out all the problems.

Looking at Rick today, it is hard to believe that he had the same difficulties most teenagers have. He was painfully shy, so much so that his first gigs were played with his back to the audience.

A dream comes true.

As soon as Rick's parents realized that their son would never give up, the fights stopped. They knew Rick's interest in music was a grown-up commitment, not a childish fad.

A few problems could not be solved at home, or by playing the guitar. Rick became very withdrawn. "I went to a psychiatrist for help," he told *Seventeen* magazine. "I didn't go to school much, and I read insatiably. . . . I also played the guitar." The psychiatrist helped him pull himself together and gain confidence.

Girls were never much of a problem—if he could get up the courage to talk to them. Once he needed a push from his friends to have enough confidence to speak to a girl he liked. And what a push it was!

"I was maybe sixteen and very shy," he wrote in answer to a question posed by a member of his first fan club. "I liked this girl at school. My friends and I were at a party one night and her boyfriend had just taken off with someone else and she was in the bedroom crying. My friends chased me for three blocks, caught me and threw me, bodily, into the room with her. I landed on the floor in front of her. Luckily, it could only have gone up from there and I dated her for about six months."

Rick is thankful that Australia did not have a drug culture when he was growing up. He had a lot of trouble fitting in with kids his age. If they had put pressure on him to take drugs, he might have done something he did not want to do, out of weakness. He told *Circus* magazine, "I remember smoking [cigarettes] because of peer pressure. I smoked for about two weeks . . . it hurt my throat to sing when I smoked, so I just said, 'Forget it.' I learned a lot about peer pressure [from moving so much and having to adapt]. I don't think I learned to beat it, but to understand it."

What did Rick learn? He learned that you cannot let your friends think for you. You feel better about yourself when you make your own decisions.

The First Taste of Success

A few years ago it seemed as if Rick Springfield came from nowhere. He starred on "General Hospital" as Dr. Noah Drake. His songs were on the radio. But Rick is not an overnight success. Years of hard work lay behind him.

At the age of seventeen Rick quit school. He joined a local band called Rock House. Rock House was quite a popular band in Australia, but there were not enough places to play. When the boys were offered a chance to tour Vietnam and entertain the troops, they decided to do it.

The Vietnam War took place in deep, rainy jungles. The band made money, but spent most of it trying to forget the horrors of the war. The members of Rock House found themselves in the middle of the action. They lived in tents, and sometimes they were under fire. Everyone was lonely and far from home. The band members and the soldiers were about the same age, and Rick identified with the soldiers and felt very sorry for them. Now that he knew what a war was like, he hoped he would never have to fight in one.

By the time he got back from Vietnam, Rick felt more confident and experienced as a musician. He could sing, and play bass, guitars, and keyboards. He wanted to work with other musicians on his own original material.

His next band, Wackedy Wak, did not last long. After that band broke up, he began again with a group called Zoot. (Rick is not the only person from Zoot to have worldwide hits. Some of the other members are now in the Little River Band.) Finally, Rick could sing his own compositions. It would be hard to recognize them, though—Zoot was a heavy metal band.

Zoot soon became the most popular of the local Australian bands. Rick won awards for his songs and his guitar skill. At last he had a taste of the success he wanted so badly—people were dancing to his music. Still, he wanted to reach more people. He knew that Australia was too small to hold his big talent.

"At the time there was no movie industry nor any significant record business," Rick told the *New York Daily News*. "You'd play Sydney and Melbourne for eighty bucks and there were three other cities you could go to if you had the plane fare. The company would put your records in an envelope and send them to England and America and that was the end of it. Top bands would vie for a shot at a ticket overseas, but they'd all bomb once they got there. That was bad for the Australian ego. We were always about three years behind the times.

"I always knew I had to come over here."

Rick's paid ticket to America came none too soon. It came from a solo single called "Speak to the Sky."

Off to America

In 1971 Zoot broke up, and Rick began recording on his own. Then, suddenly, at age twenty-two, Rick had his first No. 1 single in Australia. That single, "Speak to the Sky," caught an American record company's attention. Capitol Records signed the young singer/composer. His dreams were coming true—he could finally leave Australia. But success was not all sweet.

Not only did Rick have to leave his mother, father, and brother behind, but also a very special girl.

"It was agony," he told *Teen* magazine. "I wanted to be with her constantly and I never got anything done. I stopped writing songs. It was total involvement. But when I left and she stayed behind we just grew apart from each other."

However sad it was to leave his loved ones behind, Rick could draw comfort from his music. His first stop on the way to America was a place he had been before—London, England.

In London he recorded *Beginnings,* his first album. A new version of "Speak to the Sky" from the album eventually got into the top 15 on America's singles chart.

"Speak to the Sky" will always be a special song for Rick. One day he saw a man named Lonnie Donegan perform it on television. He had often listened to Lonnie when he was young. Hearing the famous English singer crooning his song was a wonderful experience.

When the recording ended Rick traveled to America, where a whole new life awaited him. The size of America shocked him. People coming to our country for the first time are often surprised at the size of it. He told *TV Guide* about his trip home from the Los Angeles airport. "I was no naive I spent the whole ride to my hotel playing with the electric windows on my manager's Cadillac." He can laugh about it now, but back then it was flabbergasting. There were more radio stations in California than in the whole country of Australia.

At this point, Rick lost control over his career. His managers started running it for him.

What do managers do? Managers are employed for several things. They keep track of business matters and money. They arrange personal appearances. A manager is a trouble-shooter. He or she keeps the star from getting bogged down with the little details so that the star can get on with the job—entertaining people.

Managers also take care of promotion. They keep their star in the papers, and they help bridge the gap between the public and the star. It is a difficult job. Imagine that you are Rick Springfield's manager. Besides doing all the things mentioned above, you are being trusted with something even more important—Rick trusts you with the way the public sees him. If he is too busy to make a decision himself, you have to think for him.

Rick's experience as a musician did not prepare him for the big, new world of America. Everything began happening very fast.

The managers decided to sell Rick to a teen/pre-teen audience. The teen market is huge. In the early '70s, stars such as David Cassidy and Donny Osmond were making millions as teen idols. Why not just sell Rick as a pretty face?

There were many reasons, because Rick has much more going for him than his looks. Any Rick Springfield fan knows that today. But things were different then.

One difference is the way kids are now, compared to the way they were in the early '70s. At that time, most young girls liked "bubblegum" music. Bubblegum music is soft and sappy. Girls

A smile for his
new fans
in America, 1972.

An early publicity
shot, 1972.

would go out in droves to buy a record just because the singer
was cute. These days, kids are more informed. They can read
about musicians in other magazines besides teen magazines,
because more people are interested in music, so they are
exposed to more kinds of musicians. The teen audience still has

its stars, but teens and pre-teens share them with people of other ages.

Back in the early days of Rick's career, being a teen idol told the rest of the world that you made a certain kind of music. Girls who bought Rick's records were sometimes disappointed, because they thought they were buying bubblegum music. Rick Springfield has never made just one kind of music.

He found that many people were not giving him a chance. They thought he got by on his looks alone. You will find that when people make snap judgments, they are often wrong. People thought that Rick could not be a good musician because he is handsome; which is as silly as saying that because a girl is beautiful she must be dumb.

Rick began fighting with his managers. He wanted more than pictures of himself in print. He wanted to find his audience. He knew that the teens who liked his records wanted to read more about his music.

The press coverage he got in the beginning still haunts him. People are always reminding him that he started as a teen idol. Rick is afraid to do interviews with some magazines these days, but those magazines are changing too, and in a couple of years Rick will probably be confident enough to talk to them again. He explained his press problems in *Teen* in 1982: "I'd think I was doing in-depth articles with magazines, but later I'd end up reading about my dream girl or favorite color. People would come up and say, 'I love your album but too bad it's not like Donny Osmond's.'"

He also told *Circus* magazine, "They latched onto the face without the music, and that wasn't what I came over here for. I came over to pursue a music career; I didn't come over to be a model. I want to make sure that people listen to the music; that's real important to me."

Rick cares about his fans. He has a special place in his heart for the younger ones, because they are so enthusiastic. He knows that his fans, whatever their age, love his music as much as his face. He would not have it any other way.

Rick's Magic Music

Rick's music is his own, but it is also for you.

Some of Rick's songs are very personal. He knows that by writing a song, he is sharing a personal experience with everyone who hears it. He stays close to his fans by writing lyrics about familiar things and emotions everyone shares.

Many Rick Springfield compositions are about love. Love is a big thing. It is something everyone feels. No one falls in love the same way. Rick likes to talk about love a piece at a time, so that each song is a separate little love story. He hopes that each person who hears these love stories will be reminded of his or her own feelings.

He takes great care with lyrics. It is difficult to write words that fit into the song, sound right, and get the idea across. Some words sound right when you say them and not when you sing them. Rick takes words that other people are afraid to use and puts them in songs. He likes to use words that are uncommon in rock 'n' roll. By experimenting and twisting them around, he makes them fit. Rick knows that there is no substitute for certain words when you only have a few lines to get your meaning across.

Rick shares his feelings through his lyrics.

And the music? The Rick Springfield style fits into different categories. His No. 1 single, "Jessie's Girl," topped both the pop and rock charts. His ballads are lovely. Some of his newer songs have a reggae beat. Rick takes all his influences and combines them into something all his own.

How America Became Home

Rick had immigration problems when he arrived in America. Every country has laws about the people who arrive from other countries to live and work. The number of people who immigrate is controlled. The governments want to make sure no one gets stranded, or starves, so the customs officials check people coming over the border. They look at how much money they have. If it is not enough, they sometimes send them back to their own countries.

America's immigration laws are set up to protect this country. If there is a high unemployment rate, people are discouraged from coming to look for work. Most people are let in, however, and it is very rare that someone is turned away. It is much harder to get permission from the United States government to live in America as a citizen.

Rick did not have a green card. A green card is a piece of identification the American government gives you when you become a naturalized citizen. It allows you to live and work in America permanently. Every few months, Rick made a trip over the Canadian border. Each time he went through customs his visa would be renewed and he could stay in the U.S. for a few more months.

Sounds very complicated, doesn't it? The situation certainly complicated Rick's career. Getting together a band and going on tour were almost impossible goals. "Speak to the Sky" had nothing but a pretty face to back it up. Fans did not have a chance to see Rick display his talent.

Rick had to interrupt what he was doing for those trips over the border. They broke up his life. But one of the trips solved the problem forever. During that trip, Rick lost his passport. What a disaster! He didn't know what to do. One of the people who worked for his publicist knew a man in the immigration department, who cut through all the red tape and got Rick a green card.

So the U.S.A. is now Rick's home. The California sun suits him. He loves jogging and exercise. You can tell how health-conscious he is just by looking at him. He is happy here, and we are happy to have him.

Comic Book Heroes

By the time Capitol Records released his next album Rick realized he was in trouble. His second album, *Comic Book Heroes,* continued to develop his special sound, but Capitol wanted a bubblegum sound and a bubblegum star. *Comic Book Heroes* did not sound like bubblegum music, but the label promoted it as bubblegum anyway.

This disgusted Rick. Everyone controlled Rick Springfield except Rick Springfield. He decided he would fire his managers.

It was a big step. Rick's managers also controlled his private life. They paid his bills and his rent, and they kept track of his money. Rick had never learned how to handle those things himself. Suddenly, he felt like a kid again, a kid alone and far from home.

Firing managers sounds easy, but it wasn't. Managers and their clients have a special kind of relationship. It is not the same as being a waitress and a restaurant owner. A manager and a client are more like partners, and like partners, they have contracts.

Unfortunately for Rick, his managers had not broken any of the agreements in the contract, so he had to take them to court to get out of the partnership. While his case was being heard, Rick could not work for anyone. He could not sign a new record contract, or put out any records with his name on them. When the case ended, he still could not release any records.

Rick got rid of his managers, but he had no career. The case left him $100,000 in debt. Because of all this, there was to be a three-year gap between his second album and his third.

Comic Book Hero

How Rick Became an Actor

Depressed and in debt, Rick tried his best to get along. He made clay figures and sold them at the Pasadena Swap Meet. His mom and dad sent him money. He had to pawn most of his guitars to pay the rent. A thoughtful girlfriend took him over to her parents' house occasionally for home-cooked meals.

This was to be one of the lowest points in Rick's life. He thought about going back to Australia, but he did not want to go back a failure. His friends were a big help. Rick feared that he had lost his one chance for success, but they convinced him otherwise.

Some of Rick's friends were actors and actresses, and they knew he would make a good actor. Rick did not need much convincing. He just wanted to do something creative. If he was not allowed to be a singer, he would be an actor for a couple of years.

First he had to take acting lessons. One of his coaches had starred in one of his favorite movies, *A Clockwork Orange*. The coach's name was Malcolm McDowell. *A Clockwork Orange* is a scary film about life in the future. The country is run by youth gangs, corrupt police, and a power-hungry government. McDowell plays a gang member who loves to beat up people and listen to classical music. The government conditions him with a drug to hate violence. The drug makes him ill, while the officials show him horrible movies of people getting beaten up. After the treatment he can never see violence without feeling sick, but unfortunately, some of the movies he is shown have classical music in the background. The film has a surprise ending. Malcolm McDowell's performance is excellent, and it inspired Rick to have him for a teacher.

Rick never forgot his first love, his music. While he studied acting he worked on new songs. He wanted to be ready when he got his next shot at stardom.

The young actor, 1974.

Rick in 1975.
Is this the private
life he is so
secretive about?
No, it's just a wild
outfit for an early
concert!

Wait for Night

After a three-year forced retirement, Rick was free. His management and record contracts were settled. He could sign with a new record company and start putting out albums again. A small company, Chelsea Records, signed Rick after hearing what he had been working on at home.

Wait for Night, the third Rick Springfield album, featured Nigel Olsson and Dee Murray, two musicians who played with Elton John. You can hear them on most of Elton's early hits. Nigel plays drums and Dee plays bass. They have been together for years, and are quite a rhythm section.

Rick made a good album. The radio stations were playing it, and things looked bright for the first time in years. Then, in the middle of a tour to promote the album, Chelsea Records went out of business.

Again, bad luck had spoiled Rick's bid for American stardom. This time he was not going to take it lying down.

Rick with an old four-legged friend in 1976.

"Lunch Time"

Rick knew he had to do something to change his luck. He had studied acting and worked hard at it. Maybe he could be successful as an actor. It was worth a try.

There are thousands of actors in California, and not enough acting jobs, so Rick and his girlfriend put their heads together. They wanted to find a way to stand out in the crowd of hopefuls.

That girlfriend is now an ex-, but she gave Rick two important things: his dog, Ron, and the idea for a one-act play called "Lunch Time."

Rick and his girlfriend rented a little theater and got to work. Sets were built, costumes were created, and the wheels started turning. They invited all their friends and every casting person and theatrical agent they could think of to see the play. It featured Rick as a furniture salesman who thinks he is a playboy.

An agent from Universal Pictures showed up. He saw Rick's star quality and signed him to a two-year contract. Contract actors appear in many different projects for the company that signs them, and they are paid a salary whether they work or not. Some of Rick's problems were over, but he still had a shattered career to put back together.

Rick's Television Roles

While under contract to Universal, Rick appeared in episodes of many familiar television shows. Here is a list of some of them, so you can watch for the reruns.

"The Six Million Dollar Man"—"Rollback." Rick is the villain in this one. He is on a roller derby team, the T-Birds, who are really a front for a gang. Rick fights with the Bionic Man and is put in the hospital. The Bionic Man takes his place and saves the world from the bad guys. During the filming, Rick slipped and ended up with a real black eye.

"The Nancy Drew Mysteries"—"Will the Real Santa Claus . . ." This time Rick is a sharp lawyer from Boston who comes to help in a case. The case involves a man dressed as Santa Claus who is robbing houses. Nancy and the lawyer capture the bad guy. If you see "The Nancy Drew Mysteries," you may recognize the woman who stars as Nancy. She is Pamela Sue Martin from "Dynasty."

"Wonder Woman"—"Screaming Javelins." In this show, Rick plays the college boyfriend of a Russian gymnast who is kidnapped by a maniac. The kidnapper tells the gymnast that if she does not join his Olympic team, he will kill her. The boyfriend tries to rescue her, but he is caught. Wonder Woman saves the gymnast and her boyfriend. In the happy ending, they get married.

Farrah Fawcett, move over!

"The Rockford Files"—"Dwarf in a Helium Hat." Rick has a small part, but it is a good one. He plays an English rock star who gives a big party and throws a piano in the pool.

"Battlestar Galactica." Rick appeared in the first episode of "Battlestar." He played Lorne Greene's youngest son, who dies tragically.

Success at Last

In 1980 Rick's luck changed.

Rick signed with another record company. This one would not go out of business. It is one of the biggest in the world, RCA Records. The company was impressed by the recordings Rick made at home. He had never given up his dream.

Universal had ended its contract program, however, and Rick had not acted for six months when he signed with RCA. While he made *Working Class Dog* Rick needed an income, so he played in a bar band.

"It was good to make money for a change," he told *Seventeen* magazine, "but the smoke was suffocating. I'd come home at night with my ears ringing and my clothes smelling like I'd rolled in an ashtray and smelling of liquor."

Even though he had a recording contract, Rick feared that something would come along and take it all away again. He decided to prepare for the worst and be careful.

He ended up becoming a television star.

One day, Rick got a studio call. A talent scout had seen one of his television roles. The studio was offering him the part of Dr. Noah Drake on "General Hospital." Before he auditioned for the part, Rick had never seen a soap opera. The producer who hired Rick had no idea of what he had on his hands—a future rock star. He only knew that he had found the perfect Dr. Drake.

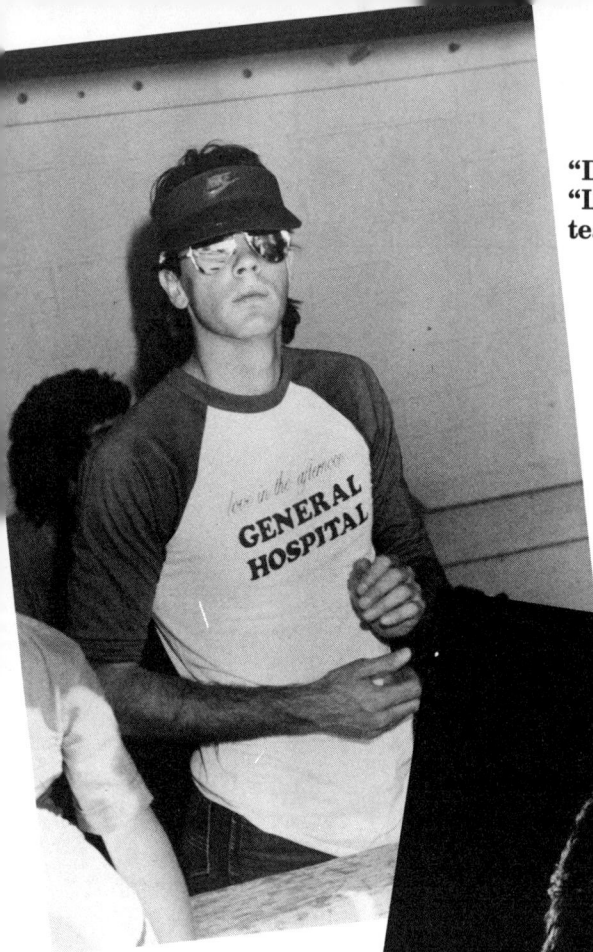

"Dr. Drake" on the "Love in the Afternoon" team.

The face and voice of 1981, the *Working Class Dog* tour.

Rick did not take chances. He knew he needed the security "General Hospital" offered. No more playing in bars. No more selling his guitars. If the record took off, he would just have to juggle two careers.

And that is exactly what happened.

The *Working Class Dog* album gave everyone a first glimpse of Rick's dog, Ron. Ron is a mix of pit bull terrier and Great Dane. He appears on the cover of the album, dressed in a shirt and tie, with a picture of Rick in his pocket. Rick had some trouble convincing RCA to put a picture of his dog on the cover of his record. The company thought that Rick's picture should go on the front.

Rick went home to make a sample cover, to show the company how great it would look. He needed a new shirt for Ron, because his neck is smaller than Ron's. "Originally I bought a shirt for myself," he told *Seventeen* magazine. "Then I went back and said I'd like the same shirt with an eighteen-and-a-half-inch neck. They sent me next door to the big man's store, where the salesman said, 'Sure, what sleeve length?' 'Doesn't matter,' I told him, but he said he needed some idea. 'Twelve inches,' I said and the guy's jaw dropped. Then I added, 'It's for my dog,' so they pulled out one with short sleeves."

The funny picture of Ron convinced RCA. The company put out a first run of covers featuring Ron. Then somebody changed his mind, and a few hundred were put out with Rick's picture on the front and Ron's on the back. Then a lot of people started talking about the cover featuring Ron, and the company changed it back again. The few hundred albums with Rick's picture on the front will probably be collector's items one day.

Rick's luck changed over the next few months. It has stayed good ever since, except for one personal tragedy. On April 24, 1981, his father passed away. Rick told *Us* magazine, "I felt disconnected. I couldn't put it together until I had written something about it. I wanted to tell everybody: You just missed a great person."

The song is called simply, "April 24, 1981." It is on the second album Rick made for RCA, *Success Hasn't Spoiled Me Yet.* The

Who's that guy with Ron?

beautiful tune and lyrics are a monument to Rick's love for his father, but the song is also a comfort for anyone who has ever lost a parent. Norman will live forever through Rick's tribute.

Rick became very busy in 1981. Dr. Noah Drake became more and more popular. Have you ever wondered how certain people from soap operas become stars? Rick started out with a medium-sized part, and ended up as one of the show's most popular characters.

First of all, you should know about "General Hospital." In 1981, it was the No. 1 soap opera in the country. It became popular because of its twisting, exciting plot. The show featured more young people than most daytime dramas. It had the meanest villains, and everything else a good soap needs. The time slot was important too. Because it was on in the afternoon, high school students could tune in to the last half hour when they got home from school—and they did. Kids their age were on the show and it featured topics of interest to teenagers. Soon everyone had caught the "General Hospital" bug. Men started watching, and college kids. Some college kids even scheduled their classes around it!

People send fan letters to their favorite characters. Some of the letters are addressed to the actors, but most of them are addressed to the character they play. The producers read these letters, and if an actor or actress receives a lot of them, they make that performer's part bigger. Dr. Noah Drake was getting love letters from women of all ages.

Rick once described Dr. Drake to *Circus* magazine as "a wealthy surgeon who probably wouldn't have been a surgeon if his parents and his family hadn't been doctors. He's very sure about what he does, very confident of his abilities, a little egotistical. A bon vivant type."

A memorable moment from "General Hospital."

Suddenly Rick Springfield was a household name because of the playboy doctor. But at the same time, "Jessie's Girl" began creeping up the charts. The single proved that Rick had more than one talent. The handsome heartthrob proved to be a good actor and a great singer/songwriter.

"Jessie's Girl" took over the airwaves. It eventually became America's No. 1 single. The catchy, upbeat pop tune had everyone singing along. The lyrics told a true story, a story that has happened to many people.

Once Rick fell in love with his best friend's girlfriend. After thinking about it, he decided not to betray his best friend and possibly lose him, so he never told either one of them about his love. The plaintive tone in Rick's voice mirrors perfectly how someone feels when he or she cannot have something that is desired.

When you have a hit record and fans, it is essential to tour. Rick wanted to go out on the road and play, even though his schedule was so tight. He arranged to play between shooting episodes of the show. It became difficult, but he loved it. To his surprise, a lot of older women came to see him play because of "General Hospital." Sometimes Rick's energetic rock 'n' roll would be too much for them. Some of the ladies left with their hands over their ears. Others liked what they heard and danced. Those ladies liked Rick Springfield as much as they liked Dr. Drake.

One thing disappointed Rick about his return to the road. Occasionally his concerts were not as good as he wanted them to be. He felt exhausted from holding up two careers. The reviews pointed out that he was rusty and lacked energy.

Rick knew his acting could not be allowed to get in the way of his music. He still wanted to act, but not on television. Movies would be the next step.

But music came first. One of Rick's proudest moments was when he called Eileen to tell her *Working Class Dog* had won him a gold record. Another prize awarded to Rick in 1981 is the most important in music: a Grammy, which he won for "Jessie's Girl."

Daytime actor,
nighttime showman,
around-the-clock star.

A number one hit!

John Denver presented the "Best Male Rock Performance" trophy to him in front of a packed auditorium. Rick held it up, looked toward his mother, and smiled. "This is for you," he said.

Rick with his Grammy, 1981.

A Night to Remember

What is it like to go to a Rick Springfield concert? If you have ever been to one, you probably cannot wait for your next chance to catch Rick's dynamic show. He loves to perform, and it really shows.

When times were hard, Rick toured as an opening act for more popular bands. He learned to charm hostile audiences who had not come to see him. He would scan the auditorium until he found people who enjoyed his music, then he played for them. Usually his excitement would spill over into the audience, who loosened up and danced. He still works hard to win over an audience today.

Rick always looks great on stage, no matter what he is wearing. Most of his clothes come from his own designs. They look tight and fit well, but they give him freedom to move. Sometimes he wears faded denims covered with colorful bits of leather. His boots are covered with leather strings, bandannas, and strips of cloth. He looks like the world's most fashionable caveman.

The lights go down. A pulsating bass sounds in the darkness. People begin to scream. The curtain whips away with a flash of light and sound.

There stands Rick, a tall, bright star. He smiles, dances, and leaps his way through a thrilling set of hits. The music is loud, but

The curtain whips away with a flash of light and sound.

Rick belts out another great tune.

Cool, pin-striped
Springfield.

"I get excited . . ."

Rick singles out a fan on the *Sweat for Success* tour.

the screaming is louder. "I Get Excited" gets a wonderful reponse, because everyone knows that he means it. Rick kicks and sweats and spins. He runs from one side of the stage to the other. He wants to see every person in the audience. This is his chance to touch their hearts. He still plays for the people who enjoy themselves, but there are many more of them these days. When you leave a Rick Springfield show, you know he has played for you. It is a night to remember.

A night to remember.

Success Hasn't Spoiled Him Yet

"General Hospital" helped Rick in many ways. He has said that television made him a better performer. But the pace was getting him down. He knew everybody from the cast, but he had no idea what characters they played. When scripts were handed out, he tore out the pages with his lines on them and then memorized them. Reading the rest of the script confused him. Millions of people knew every detail of "General Hospital's" plot, but Rick was not one of them!

He spent his time between takes composing. His dressing room contained a little electric piano with earphones. Privacy is essential when Rick is composing. No one can hear the songs for the next album but him.

Success Hasn't Spoiled Me Yet featured Ron on the cover again. In the cover photo, Ron is dressed up and seated in a limousine between two poodles. Rick is dressed as a chauffeur and is serving champagne. Rick made the album at night after he had finished taping the show, and he still did weekend mini-tours.

Rick felt convinced of his success, so after two years of "General Hospital," he called it a day. Dr. Drake got sent to another hospital, just in case Rick changed his mind. Some of Rick's fans were disappointed when he quit the show, because they enjoyed seeing him on television so much, but Rick really needed a rest.

The great singles from Rick's fifth album pushed it to the No. 2 slot on *Billboard*'s national charts. "Don't Talk to Strangers" and "Calling All Girls" carried on what "Jessie's Girl" had begun. Rick won the American Music Award for "Favorite Male Vocalist" in 1982.

It was now time to pick a movie script. If you were a big star with a lot of scripts to pick from, how would you choose? It is not an easy decision. When you have never acted in a movie before it is even harder, because you must pick a script that will earn you a good reputation. Since people pay to see movies, the people who make them are not likely to take risks. A bad performance can set you back a long way.

Rick wanted to find the right movie. Scripts came and went. Silly rumors went around. One paper hinted that Rick would co-star with Brooke Shields, saying that he got the part because he is tall enough to look her in the eye.

Besides the right script, Rick wanted the right cast. The actors and actresses at "General Hospital" had been professionals. He knew how important good co-workers could be. Once he even did a scene with one of the greatest actresses in the world.

Elizabeth Taylor is a big "General Hospital" fan. She once made a guest appearance on the show. The first time Rick saw her, he had a peanut butter and banana sandwich in his mouth. He could not even say hello, because his mouth was gummed up. Later, he told *TV Guide* about their scene together: "I had to mumble one or two silly lines to her and after it was over she looked up at me and said, 'Sometimes acting is so stupid!' "

She is right. Acting pairs up a lot of odd couples. If you do not have a good sense of humor about the ridiculous things that you have to say and do, it can get you down.

Rick has definite ideas about the characters he wants to play. "I basically want to play characters that are themselves the way Cary Grant or Robert Redford is. I'm not some genius character actor like Robert DeNiro or Al Pacino," he told *TV Guide*.

At one point, Rick considered doing a film of a great modern horror and love story. The book is called *Interview with the*

"Calling All Girls."

The "Favorite Male Vocalist" of 1982.

Vampire. He may do it one day, but for his first movie, he picked *Hard to Hold.*

In *Hard to Hold* Rick plays a familiar role, that of a musician named James Roberts. James is involved with two women. One is a child psychologist, played by Janet Eilver. The other woman is played by Patti Hansen. You may recognize her name. She is the beautiful model who recently married Keith Richards of the Rolling Stones.

Hard to Hold is a chance to get a good look at Rick's acting skills. His director, Larry Peerce, thinks Rick can be any kind of star he wants to be. Since Rick recorded four new songs for the soundtrack, it is also a chance to hear more of Rick's great tunes.

When you see the film, you will notice that Rick has lost his accent. Actually he lost it when he started studying acting. If he had kept it, he would have been typecast, and Rick did not want to be restricted to playing Englishmen and Australians. However, he can still get his old accent back when he wants to.

Living in Oz

In 1983, Rick made a movie and album. *Hard to Hold* premiered on April 6, 1984. The album has been out for a long time. That album is *Living in Oz*. Oz is a nickname for Australia. Rick's sixth album is a big step forward for him. It is full of songs about some very emotional years. It is also the first record Rick has produced all by himself.

What does a producer do? Record producers basically run things. It is a hard job, one that takes skill and years of practice. There are thousands of little knobs in the studio, and the producer must know what each one of those knobs does, and how to use them to get the sound he wants.

Most of the records you hear are made in twenty-four track studios. This means that there are twenty-four different spaces on the recording tape. Everything is recorded piece by piece— drums go on one track, and then the bass, and so on. Finally the vocal is put on.

The producer must remember where everything is. He must know how to get exactly the sound the artist wants, and also what sounds do not work together. It took Rick years to be confident enough to produce himself. Now he plays two roles in the studio: First, he listens to what he is doing as the producer, then he listens to it as the artist.

A personal moment on the *Living in Oz* tour.

Rick wanted *Living in Oz* to be different from his previous two albums. You can spot one difference right away. The cover is just a simple portrait of Rick, looking seriously into the camera.

As a composer, Rick has always been very open. He shares his feelings through his lyrics, instead of talking about them to the press. Then it is just between him and his fans. Two of the most emotional and heartfelt songs on *Living in Oz* are "Alison" and "Me and Johnny." "Alison" is about a married woman. She and Rick fell in love. Every time he saw her husband he felt terrible. He knew their love was doomed long before they split up. "Me and Johnny" is about a boy with whom Rick grew up. Rick still stays in touch with John, who is his only remaining childhood friend. John is married now, with children, but long ago, he and Rick planned to be stars together.

There is a new twist in Rick's music. The powerful guitars are complemented by moody synthesizers. One of the best mixes of

the two is on the fantastic "Human Touch." "Human Touch" was the first of three great singles from *Living in Oz*. The next was the hand-clapping, rock-'n'-roll singalong, "Affair of the Heart." The third was the dramatic "Souls." Rick's music has not settled down as he has matured. If anything, it gets harder, faster, and better.

As you know, the music industry has been hit by video madness. Everyone wants to watch rock videos. They are a great way to get a closer look at your favorite stars. The cable station, MTV, shows music videos twenty-four hours a day.

Some performers have trouble adjusting to the new video trend. You can see it in their videos. They look stiff and uncomfortable.

Other performers feel comfortable in front of the cameras. Rick Springfield is one of the select few who is as used to cameras as to live audiences. Rick knows how to communicate through the camera. It is easy for him to be relaxed and still do a good job. Usually his videos only hint at the plot of the song and concentrate on images. The images set up a mood. Then the people watching can still imagine that the song means whatever it means to them personally. Yet they can see how Rick felt when he thought of the song.

A 1982 television appearance.

What Is Rick Like?

Millions of people know what Rick Springfield looks like. They have seen his face on "General Hospital" and in magazines. But what is Rick really like?

He admits that he is a very private person who likes having a house of his own. He told *US* magazine jokingly, "I've got to have a place where I can let go—put the zit cream on, the curlers in my hair . . . ," but he is serious about enjoying his privacy.

Rick loves his fans, but he does not like them peeking in his windows. Once he had to move because fans were following him home and camping out on his lawn. Now he lives in a more secluded area. Think about it. How would you feel if you went out to get your mail in a bathrobe and people were sitting in your driveway? You would not feel very friendly toward them. It is not the best way to show your affection for a star.

Rick spends a lot of time in the public eye. He knows that he owes his fans gratitude, but everyone deserves a private life. He does not want to be put in the position of playing the bad guy, and that is what he must do when fans invade his home.

Rick's love life is another sensitive issue. Publicity helped to break up one of his romances. A few years ago, he dated an actress named Linda Blair. She was famous for starring in a horror movie called *The Exorcist,* in which she played a twelve-year-old girl possessed by the Devil. Because Linda and Rick were both celebrities, they were plagued by reporters. The reporters forgot that they were people and treated them as merely subjects for a story. Many pictures of Rick and Linda appeared in the papers. Some of the reporters made snide

"... gentle, kind, imaginative, funny, and energetic."

comments. Finally, the two could not stand it anymore, and they broke up.

Rick does not want that to happen again, so he never tells the papers about his girlfriends. He is protecting his privacy and his relationships.

One of Rick's worst faults does not sound like a fault, but he knows what it is, and he is the first to admit it. He is much too hard on himself, and he works too hard. Things have to be done over and over again, until Rick thinks they are perfect. If no one stops him, he will work until he collapses.

Once the work piled up, and Rick realized he had bitten off more than he could chew. While he was making his second album for RCA, he was still appearing on "General Hospital," and also playing gigs on weekends. In 1982 Rick played 150 gigs and did over 100 episodes of the show. It was a mess, and Rick never wants to be that busy again.

"Muscles" Springfield works out on stage.

Because he is tough on himself, Rick is not conceited. He always thinks he can do better. Praise does not go to his head.

How did Rick manage to get through the hard times? One of the things that helps him when he is down in the dumps is positive thinking. He first heard about positive thinking when he was seventeen, when an insurance man came to the Springthorpe home and stopped in for a while. Rick did not buy any insurance, but he did become interested in the man's attitude. The insurance man told him how he managed. Positive thinking is simple. You get to your goals one step at a time, setting up small goals that lead to the big one. Every time you reach one of the little goals, you know you are getting somewhere.

When he feels depressed, Rick writes out his goals. Then he puts the papers up on the walls where he can see them all the time. He also tacks up articles and pictures, things that make him feel good. In the middle of one bad stretch, he read an article about a musician named Bob Seger. Bob had some awful times, but he pulled through. Rick read the article every day for inspiration.

When Rick is under pressure, he has a system to keep himself under control. He lets out the pressure in private. Sometimes he goes into a room and yells until he feels better. If he is still angry, he throws a pillow at the wall. This saves him from taking out all that irritation on the people he works with.

One of Rick's best qualities is his self-control. It makes him a truly admirable star, and a nice person.

We all know how important Rick's music is to him, but his fans are also important. Some people are mostly concerned with what the record company or the critics think of their music. Critical respect and credibility are fine, but they are not the most rewarding kind of admiration. Rick is happiest when he makes a record that his fans like.

People who work with Rick say he is a great guy. Jackie Zeman, who plays Bobbie Spencer on "General Hospital," described him as gentle, kind, imaginative, funny, and energetic.

A Happy Ending

Nineteen eighty-four will be a great year for Rick Springfield. *Hard to Hold* will hit the cinemas, its soundtrack and a new Rick Springfield album will hit the record racks, and Rick himself will hit the road for another tour. Yes, it is a happy ending after all. But it is an ending of only a small part of Rick's life. There is much more to come.

**Smile from
a superstar.**

Facts and Figures

NAME: Richard Lewis Springfield/Springthorpe.

BIRTHDAY: August 23, 1949.

SIGN: Rick was born on the cusp of Leo and Virgo. According to his chart he is mostly Leo.

MARITAL STATUS: Single, but he has almost been married three times.

HAIR: Blackish-brown.

EYES: Hazel or green.

HEIGHT: 6'1" barefoot.

INSTRUMENTS PLAYED: Guitar, bass, piano, banjo, harmonica.

HOBBIES: Rick's hobbies have varied over the years, but some of them have been motorbike riding, horseback riding, target shooting, clay modeling, jogging, stained glass, skiing, and hiking.

FOOD: Rick is a vegetarian. He likes animals too much to eat meat. He eats authentic Japanese food, seafood, and vegetables. Vegetarians have to follow a careful diet. They must make sure they get enough protein. Rick makes up for lack of animal protein with fish and cheese.

FAVORITE COMPOSERS: Many, including John Lennon and Paul McCartney, Leiber and Stoller, and Beethoven.

FAVORITE MUSICIANS: The list is endless, but here are some of the people Rick enjoys: the Beatles, Graham Parker, the Who, Rickie Lee Jones, Manfred Mann, Elvis Costello, Peter Gabriel, Squeeze, and Sparks.

FAVORITE MOVIES: Here are a few: *A Clockwork Orange, Forbidden Planet, Casablanca,* and *Rebel Without a Cause.*

FAVORITE SPORTS: Rick once wrote on a questionnaire, "Karate, jogging (if I can't beat 'em, I run)."

DID YOU KNOW THAT:

- Rick's second language is French. He took it in school and can still speak it a little.
- Rick did not have a driver's license until 1975. Before then he always rode motorbikes.
- There is an unreleased Rick Springfield album. Some of the songs are, "Call the Fire Brigade," "Child Within," and "Sweet Teaser."
- Ron's nickname is Lethal Ron.
- Rick used to do a song called "Bruce" in concert. It was about people confusing him with Bruce Springsteen.
- Rick appeared on another soap besides "General Hospital." He did a few episodes of "The Young and the Restless."
- Five hundred girls once stormed the backstage door of a Rick Springfield concert in Long Island. A guard's leg was broken. Rick sat with the man and talked to him until the ambulance arrived.
- One of Rick's role models is Frank Sinatra.
- Rick's brother Mike is working on his own songs in Australia.
- Rick did not tour his homeland until the "Living in Oz" tour. He also went to Japan for the first time in 1983.
- Rick sometimes gets ideas for songs in dreams. He has to wake up and write them down.
- One of Rick's least talked-about faults is his absent-mindedness.
- Besides Malcolm McDowell, two of his favorite film stars are Jane Fonda and Steve McQueen.

Rick rocks for you!

Discography

SINGLES

"Speak to the Sky"	1971
"Come On Everybody"	1973
"I'm Your Superman"	1973
"Believe in Me"	1973

ALBUMS

Beginnings   Capitol   1972
   "Mother Can You Carry Me"
   "Speak to the Sky"
   "What Would the Children Think"
   "1000 Years"
   "The Unhappy Ending" (Lead Me On)
   "Hooker Jo"
   "I Didn't Mean to Love You"
   "Come On Everybody"
   "Why?"
   "The Ballad of Annie Goodbody"

Comic Book Heroes   Capitol   1973
   "I'm Your Superman"
   "Weep No More"
   "Why Are You Waiting"
   "Believe in Me"
   "Misty Water Woman"
   "The Liar"
   "The Photograph"
   "Bad Boy"
   "Born Out of Time"
   "Do You Love Your Children"

Wait for Night   Chelsea   1975
Working Class Dog   RCA   1981
   "Jessie's Girl"
   "Love is Alright Tonight"
   "I've Done Everything For You"

Beginnings reissued by Capitol   1981
Success Hasn't Spoiled Me Yet   RCA   1982
   "Calling All Girls"
   "Don't Talk to Strangers"
   "I Get Excited"

Living in Oz   RCA   1983
   "Human Touch"
   "Affair of the Heart"
   "Souls"
   "Alyson"
   "Me and Johnny"
   "Motel Eyes"
   "Tiger By The Tail"
   "I Can't Stop Hurting You"
   "Like Father, Like Son"

Wait for Night reissued by RCA   1983
Hard to Hold soundtrack   RCA   1983